Greatest Movie Hits

Contents

Alfred

D0898831

ISBN-10: 0-7390-4112-6
ISBN-13: 978-0-7390-4112-3

AMERICA'S AVIATION HERO
(from "The Aviator")

Composed by Howard Shore
Arranged by Carol Matz

Expressively

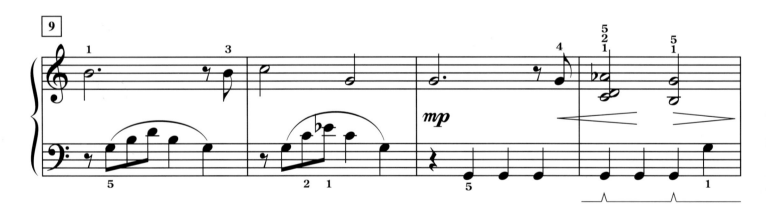

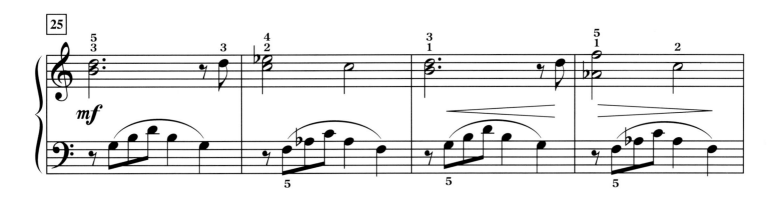

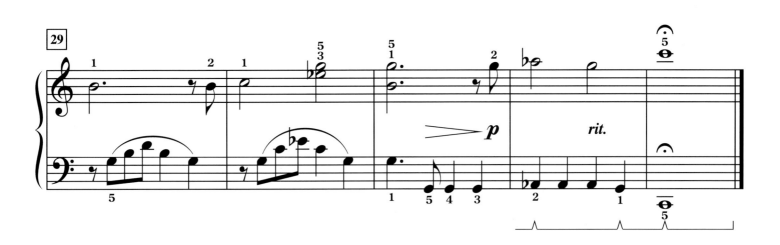

BELIEVE
(from "The Polar Express")

Words and Music by
Glen Ballard and Alan Silvestri
Arranged by Carol Matz

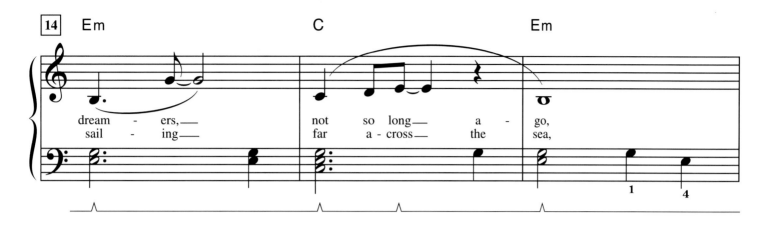

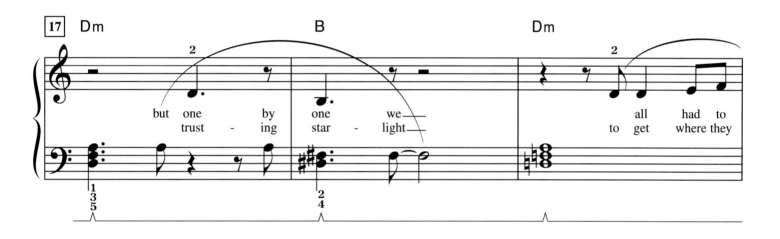

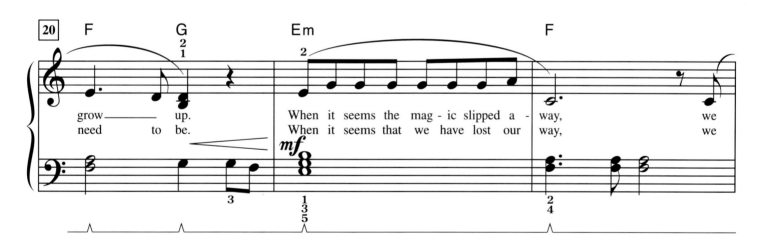

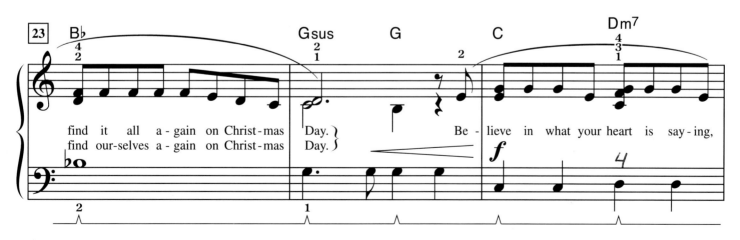

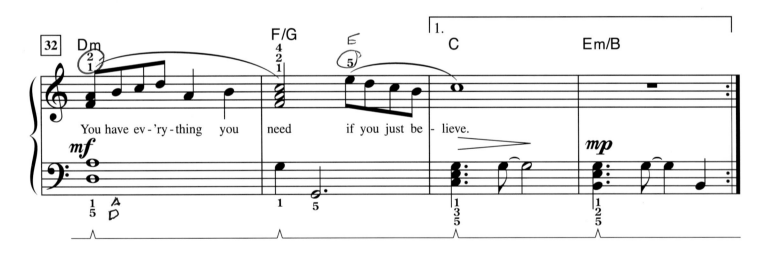

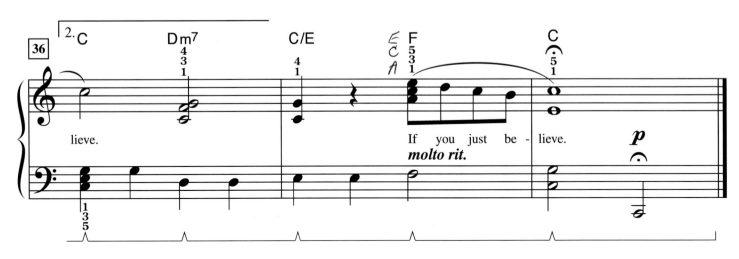

BELIEVER
(from "Be Cool")

Words and Music by
will.i.am and John Legend
Arranged by Carol Matz

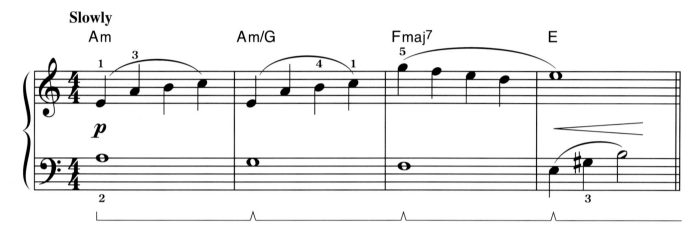

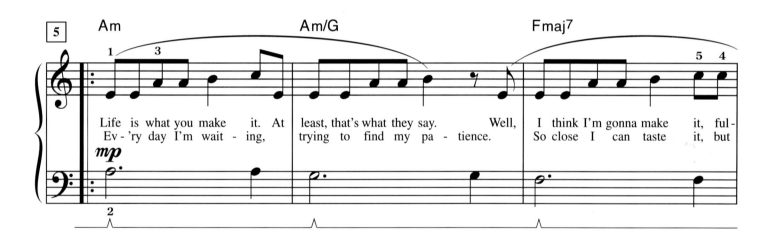

Life is what you make it. At least, that's what they say. Well, I think I'm gonna make it, ful-
Ev-'ry day I'm wait-ing, trying to find my pa-tience. So close I can taste it, but

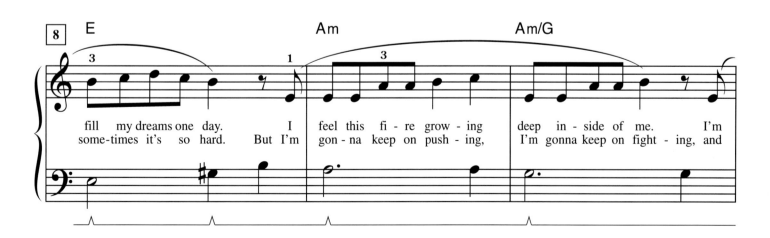

fill my dreams one day. I feel this fi-re grow-ing deep in-side of me. I'm
some-times it's so hard. But I'm gon-na keep on push-ing, I'm gonna keep on fight-ing, and

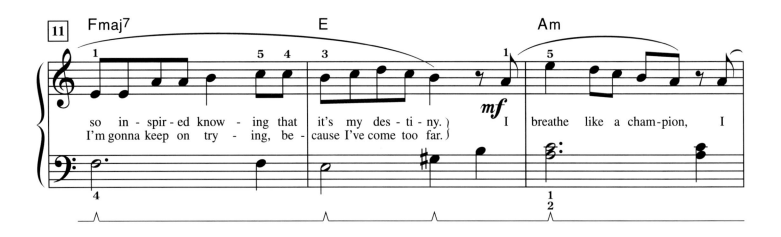

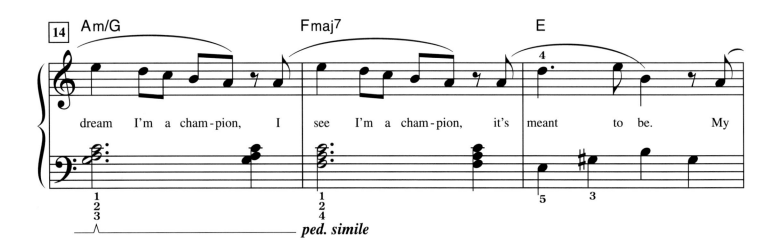

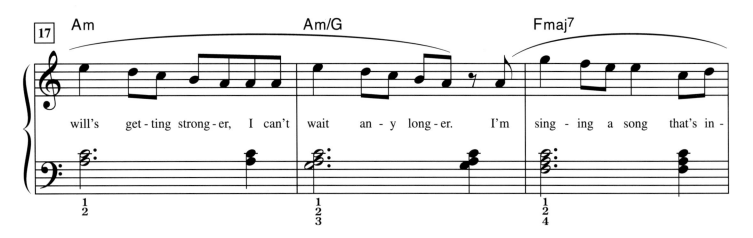

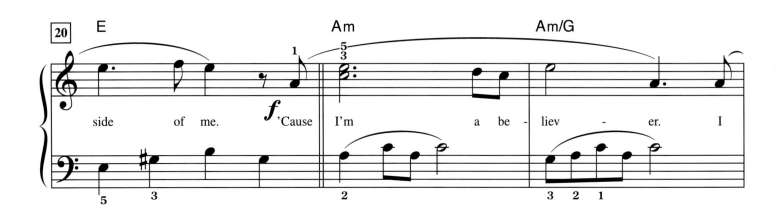

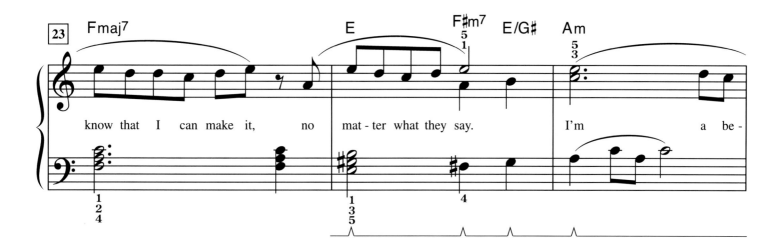

know that I can make it, no mat - ter what they say. I'm a be -

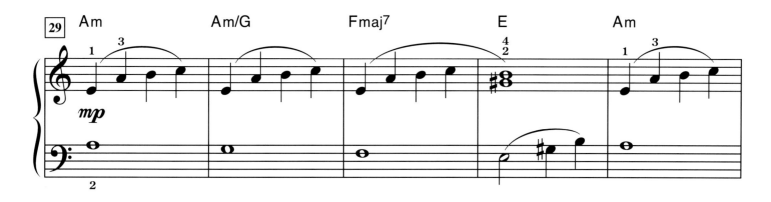

liev - er. The fu - ture is now, it____ starts____ to - day.

ped. simile

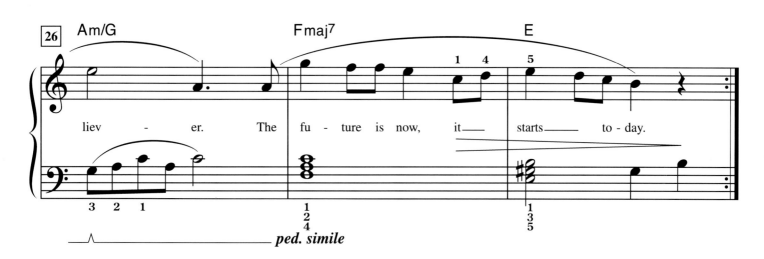

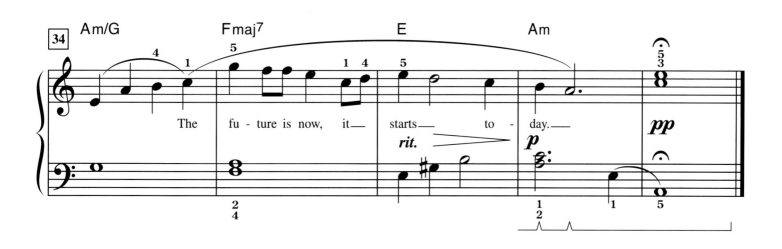

The fu - ture is now, it____ starts____ to - day.____

rit.

BREAKAWAY

(from "The Princess Diaries 2: Royal Engagement")

Words and Music by Matthew Gerrard,
Bridget Benenate and Avril Lavigne
Arranged by Carol Matz

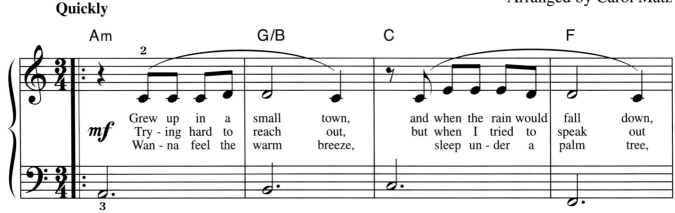

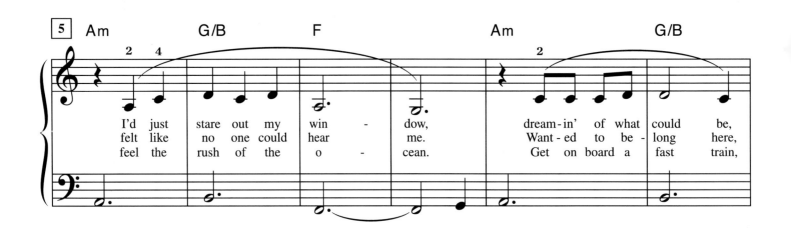

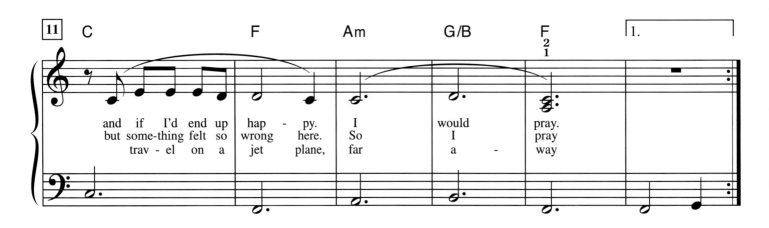

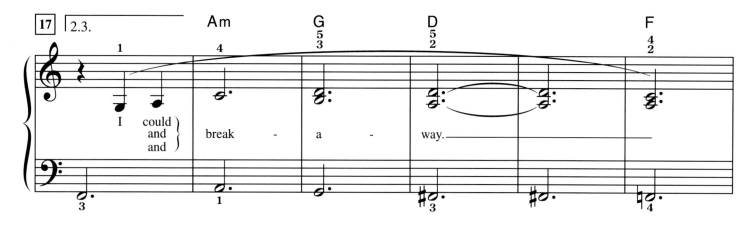

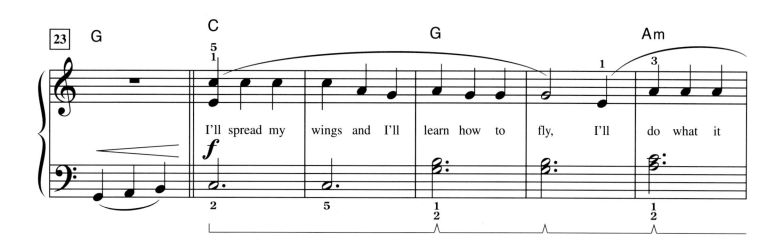

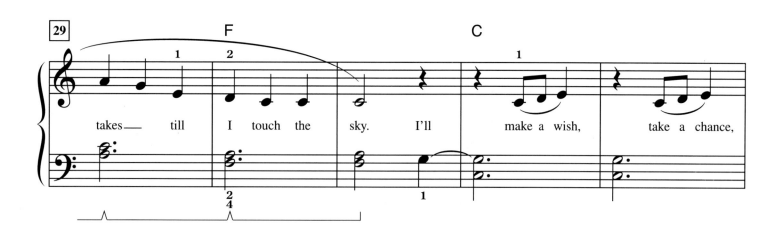

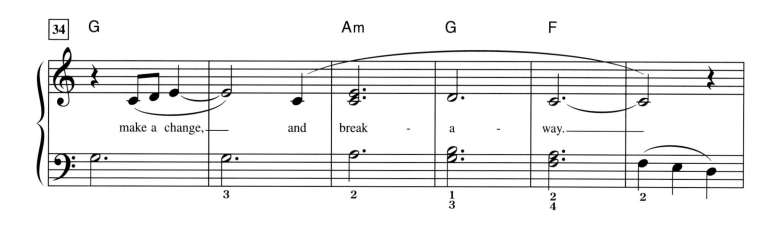

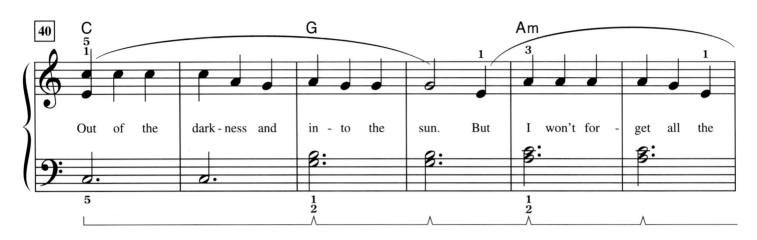

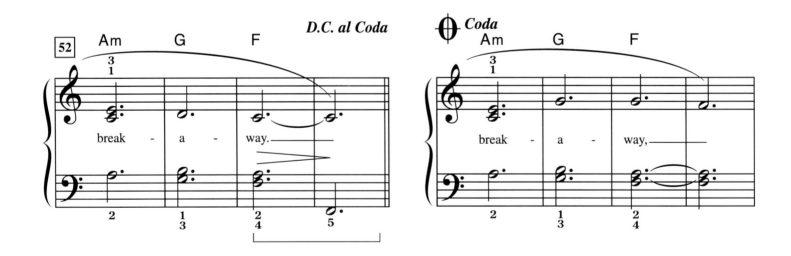

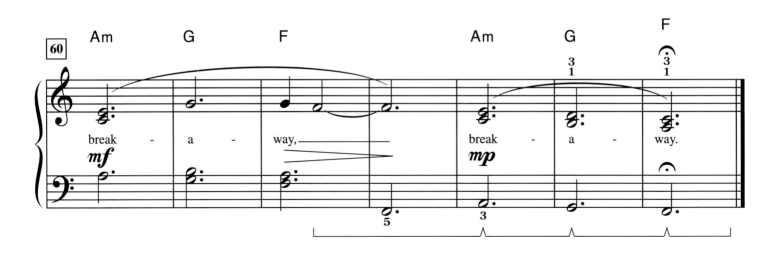

CORPSE BRIDE
(Main Title)

Music by Danny Elfman
Arranged by Carol Matz

Flowing quickly

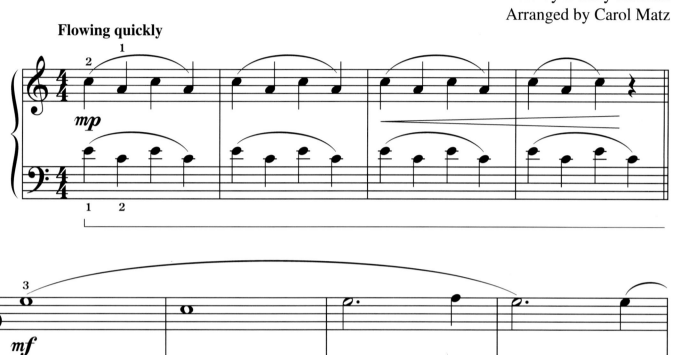

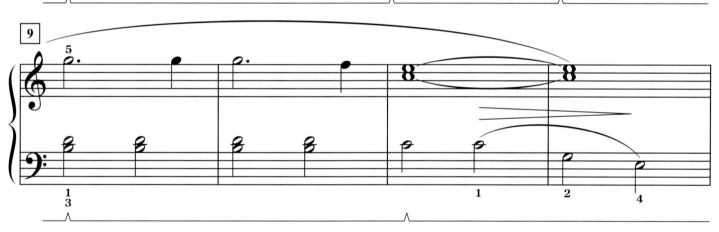

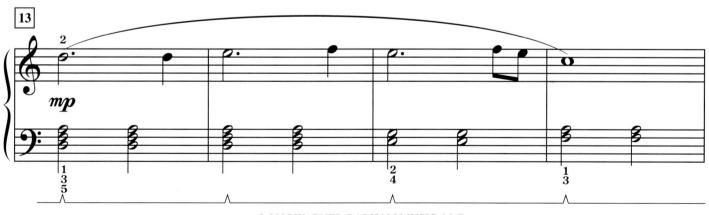

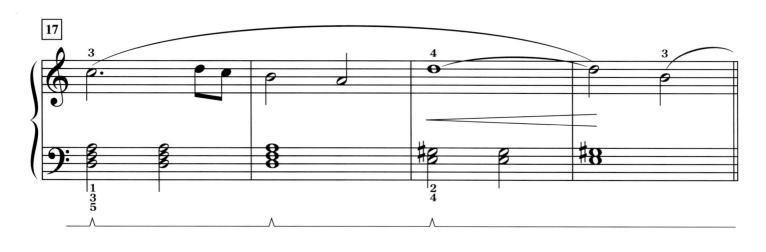

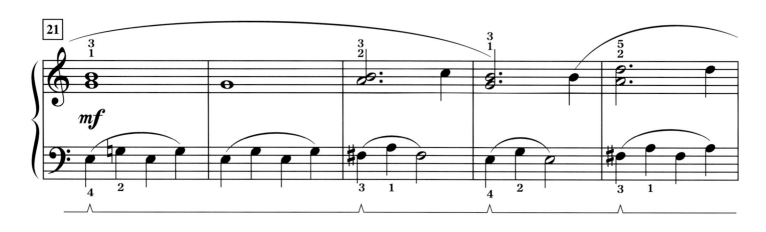

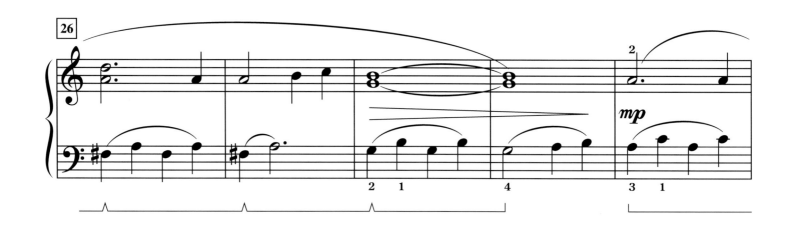

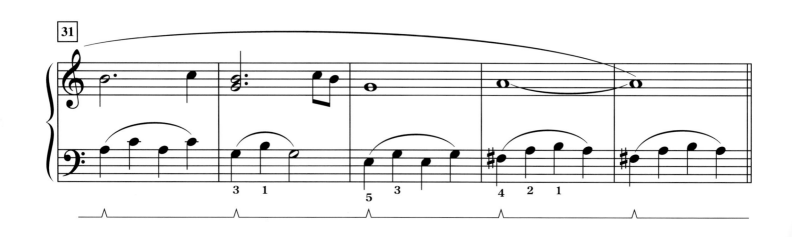

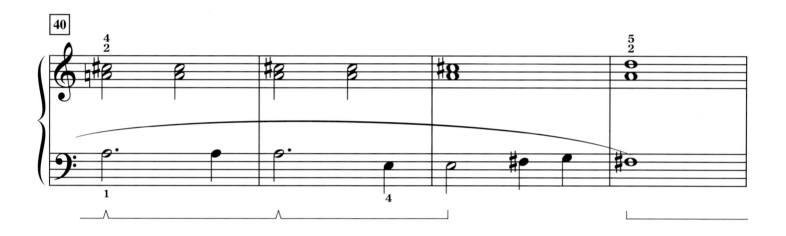

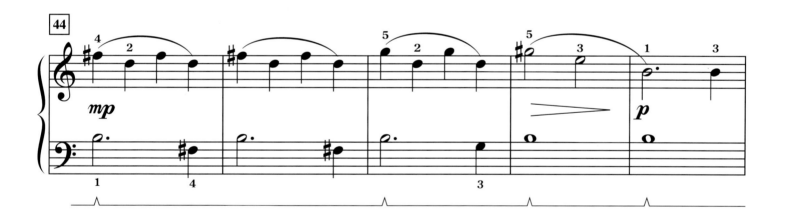

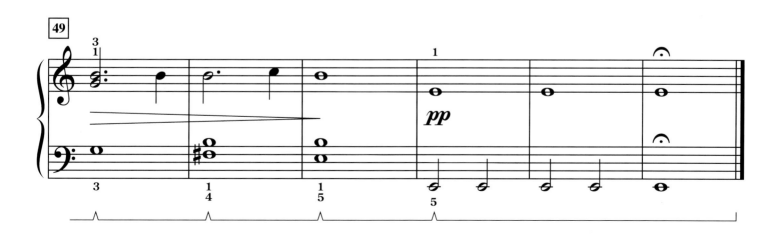

DOUBLE TROUBLE
(from "Harry Potter and the Prisoner of Azkaban")

Words and Music by **JOHN WILLIAMS**
Arranged by Carol Matz

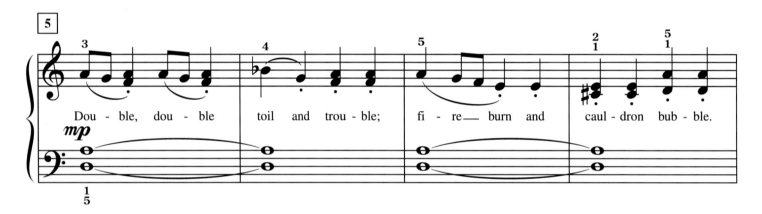

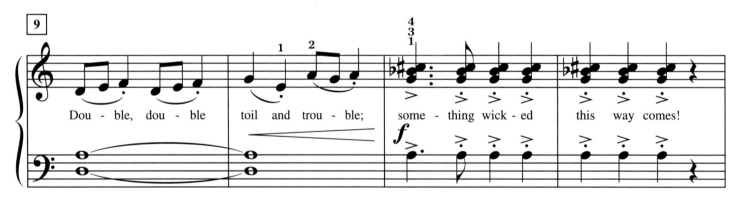

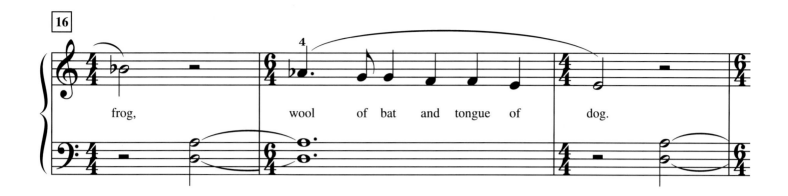

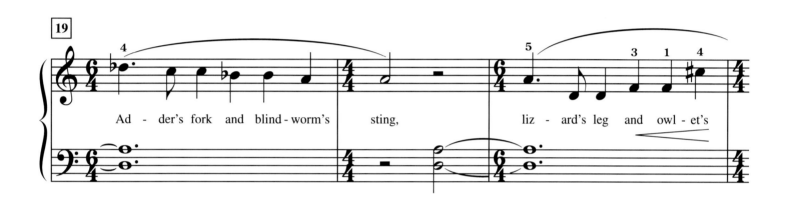

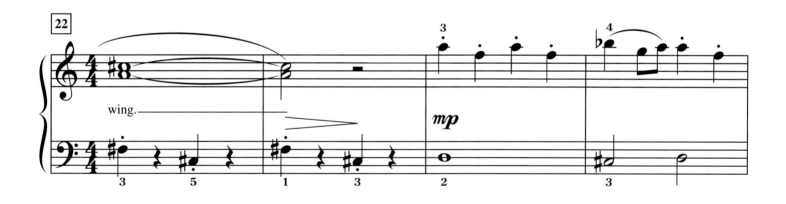

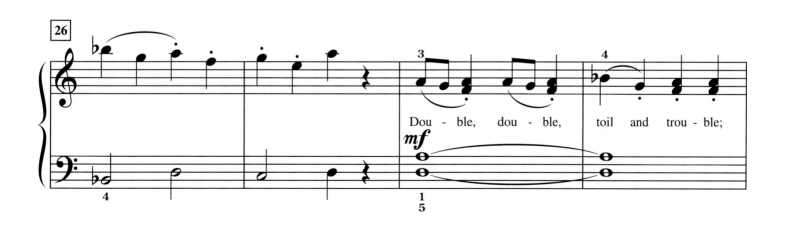

EVERYTHING BURNS
(from "Fantastic 4")

Words and Music by Ben Moody
Arranged by Carol Matz

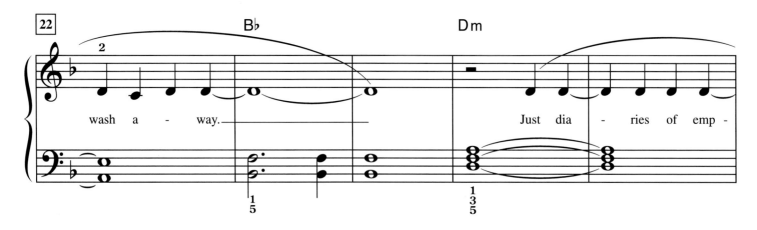

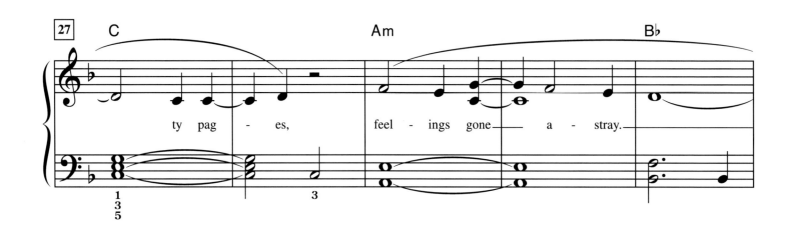

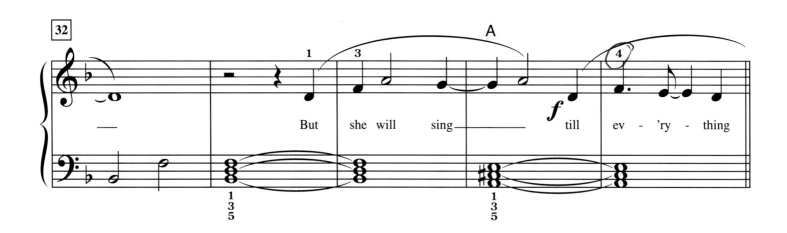

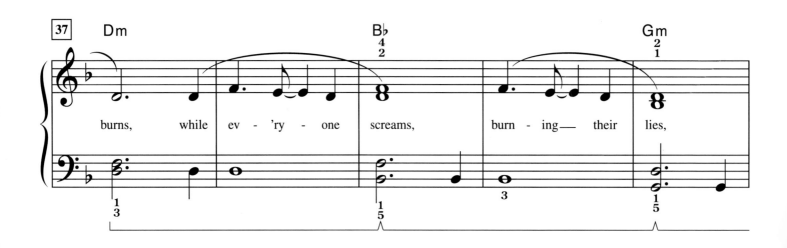

21

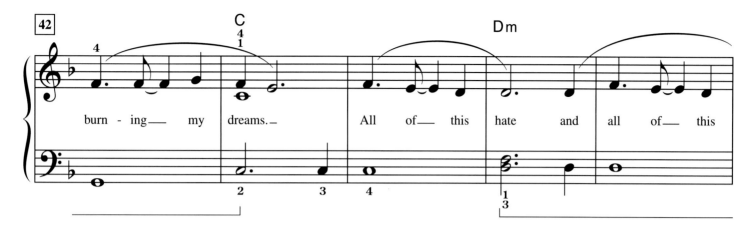

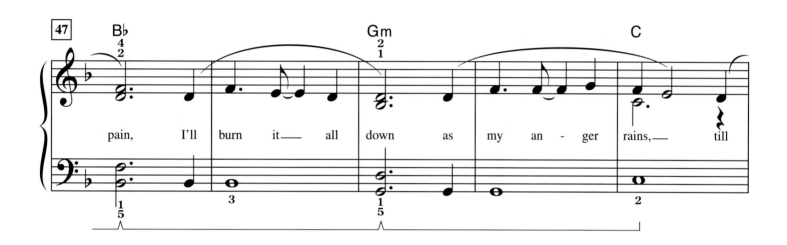

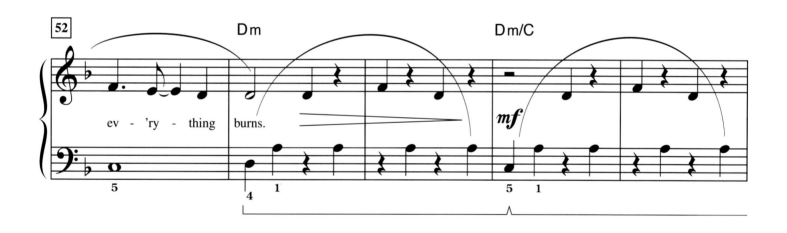

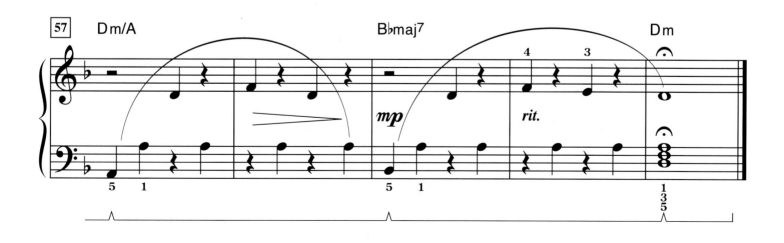

HEDWIG'S THEME
(from "Harry Potter and the Sorcerer's Stone")

Music by **JOHN WILLIAMS**
Arranged by Carol Matz

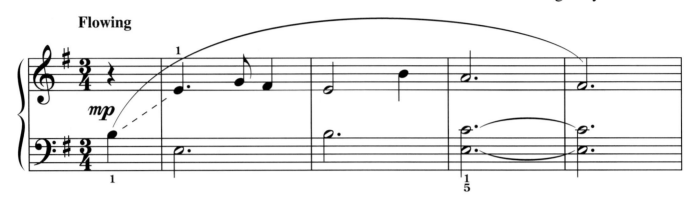

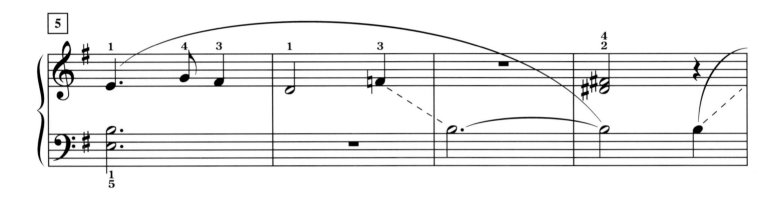

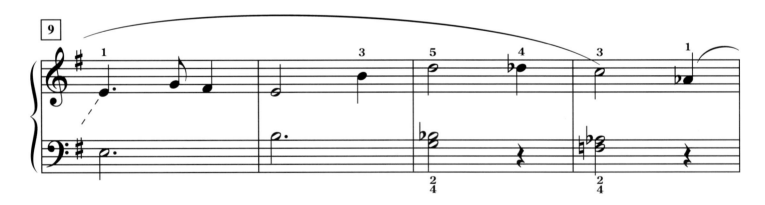

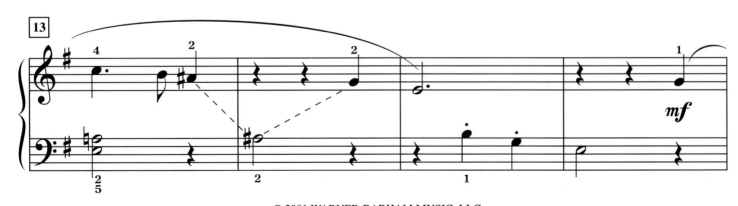

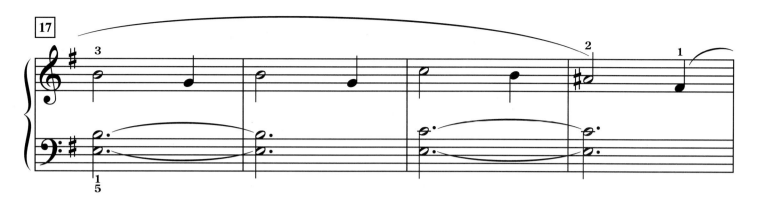

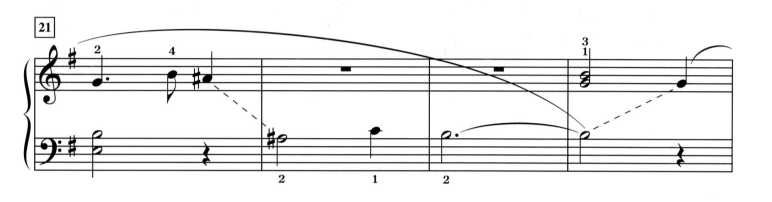

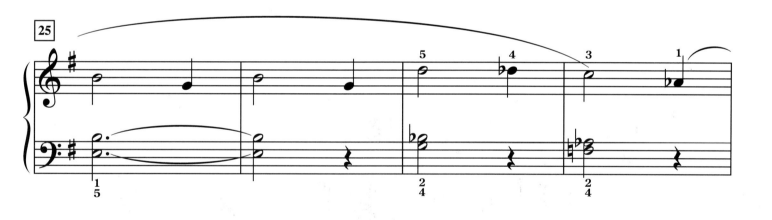

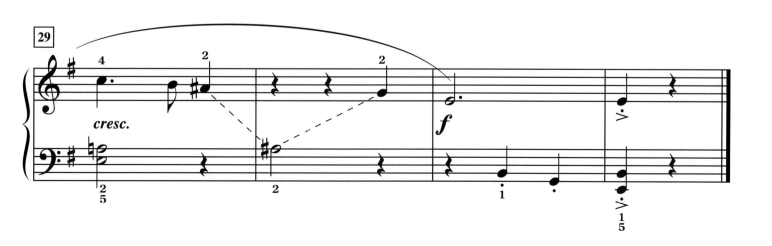

HOGWARTS' HYMN
(from "Harry Potter and the Goblet of Fire™")

By Patrick Doyle
Arranged by Carol Matz

Slowly, expressively

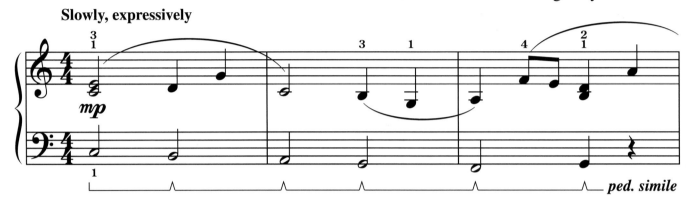

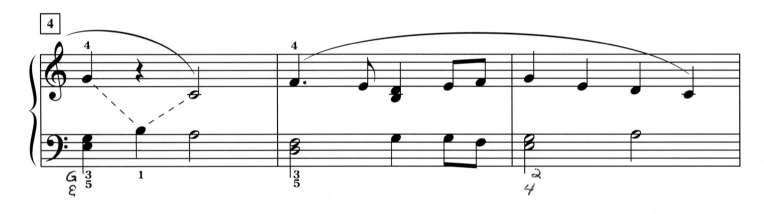

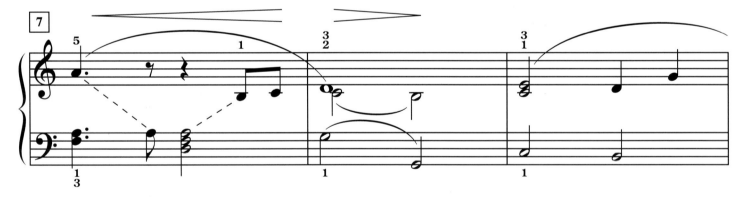

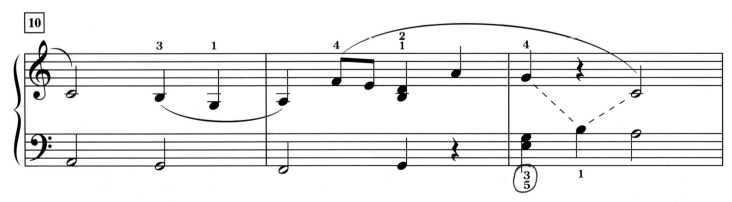

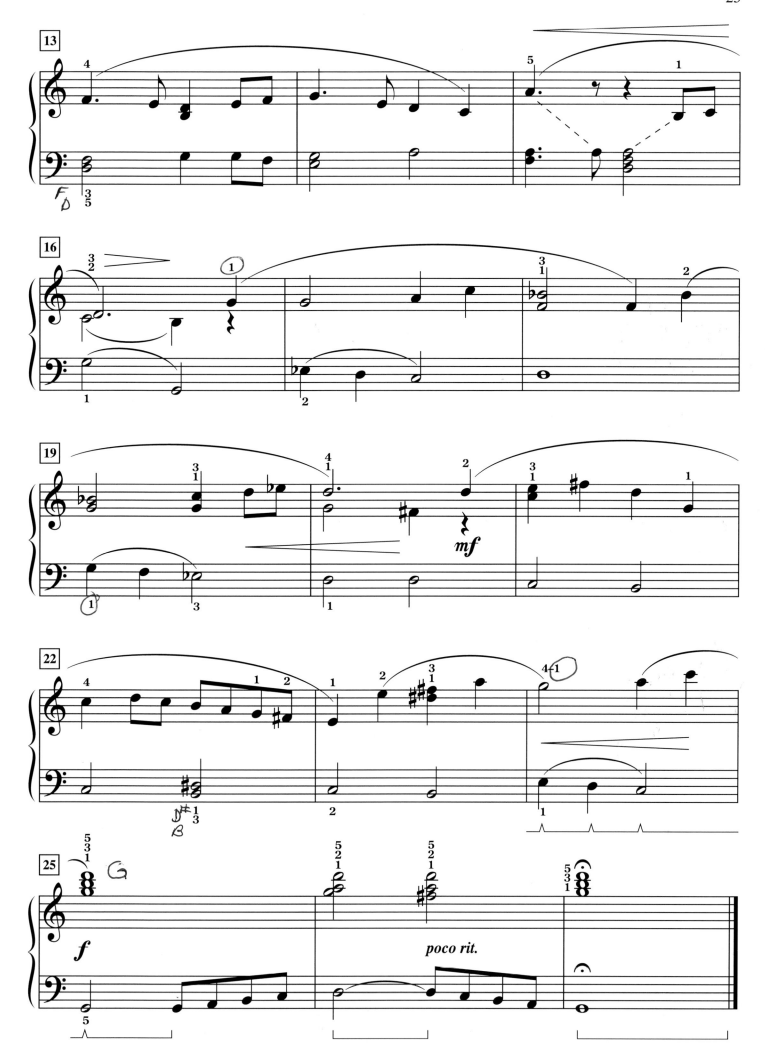

INTO THE WEST
(from "The Lord of the Rings: Return of the King")

Words and Music by Fran Walsh,
Howard Shore and Annie Lennox
Arranged by Carol Matz

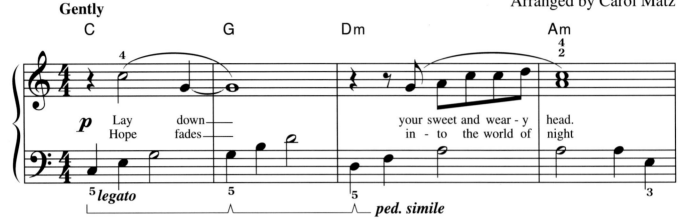

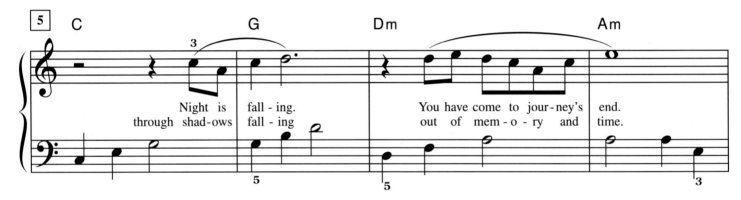

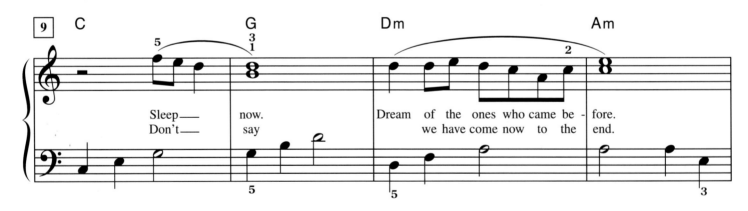

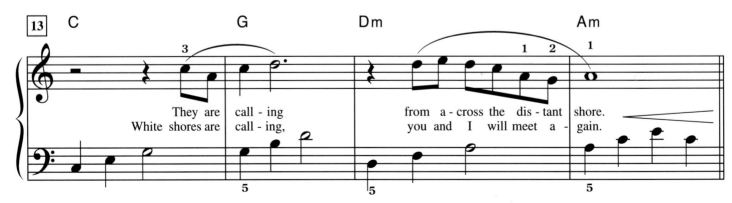

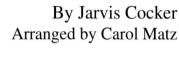
MAGIC WORKS

(from "Harry Potter and the Goblet of Fire™")

By Jarvis Cocker
Arranged by Carol Matz

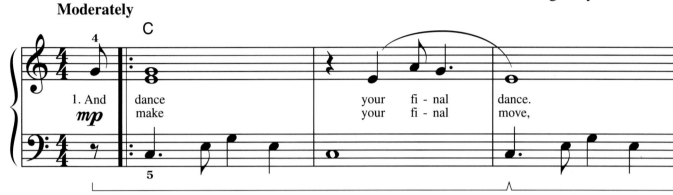

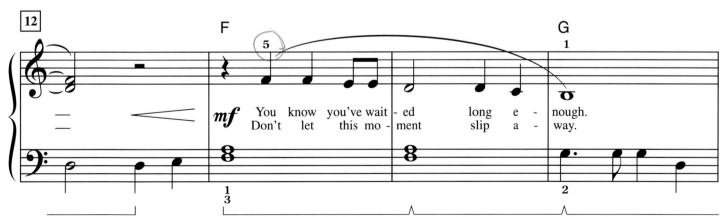

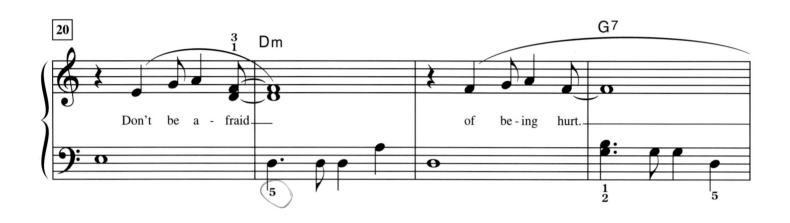

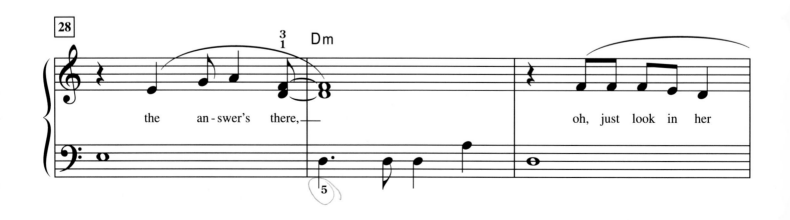

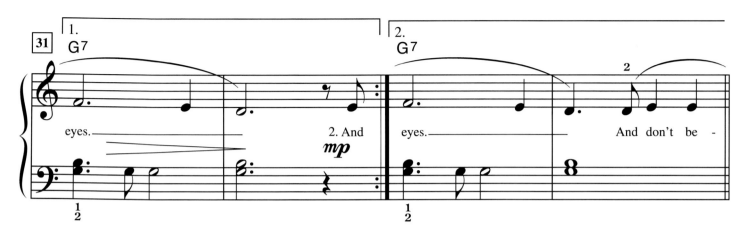

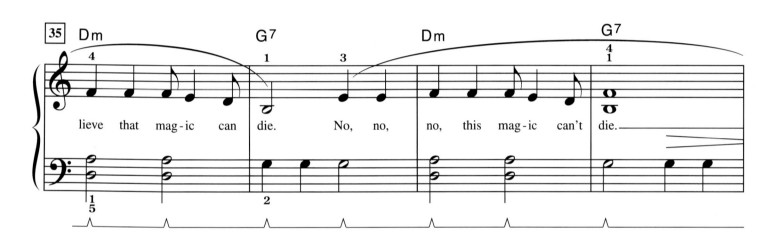

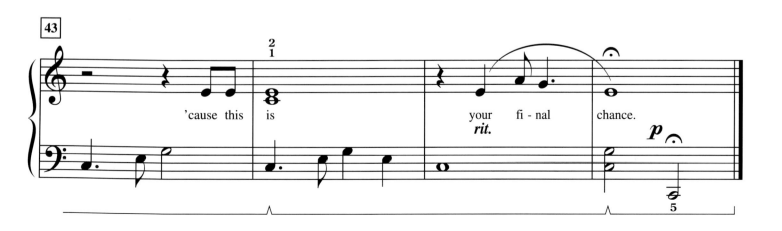

Opening Theme from

MARCH OF THE PENGUINS

(The Harshest Place on Earth)

By Alex Wurman
Arranged by Carol Matz

Moderately slow

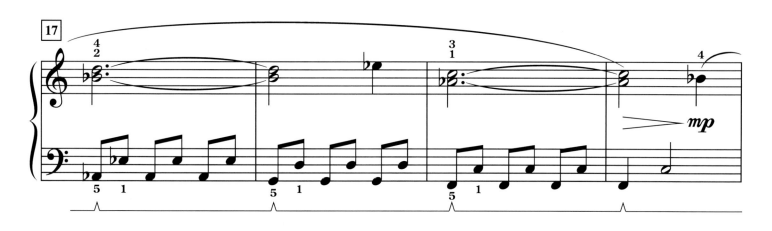

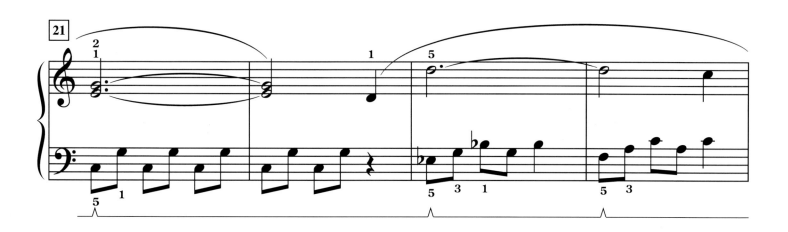

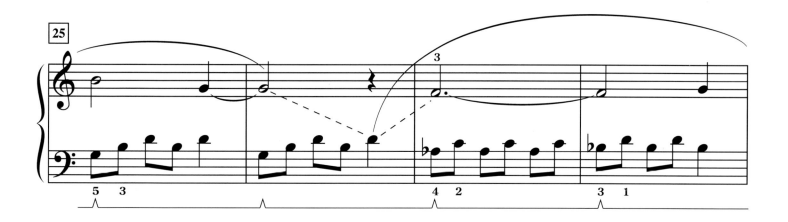

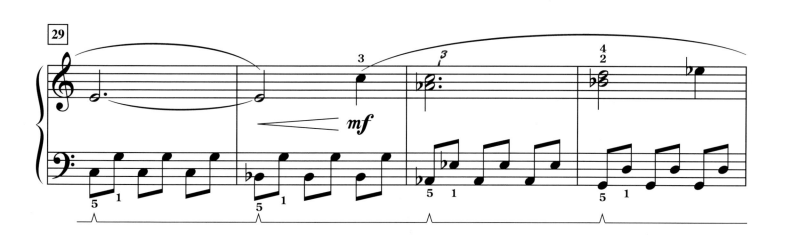

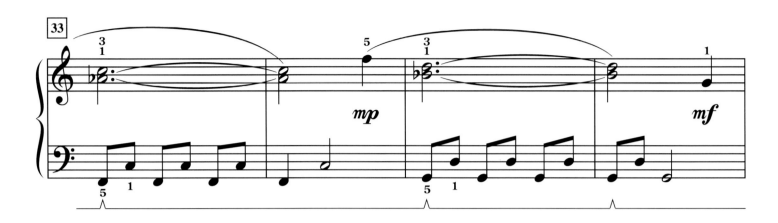

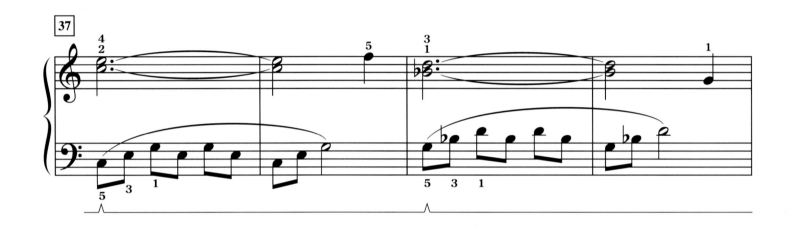

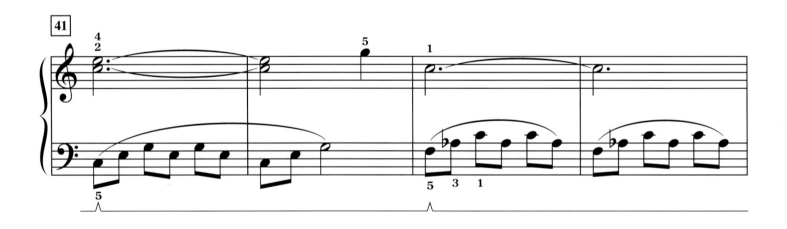

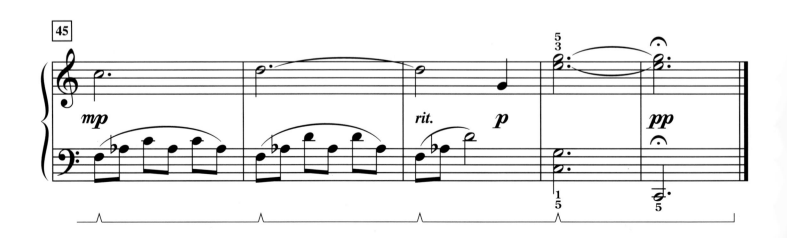

THE NOTEBOOK
(Main Title)

Written by Aaron Zigman
Arranged by Carol Matz

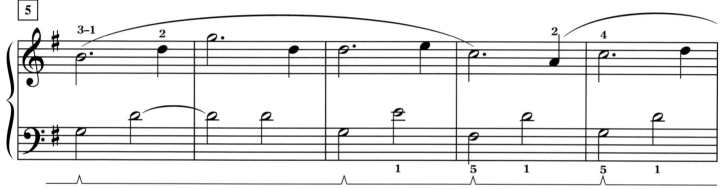

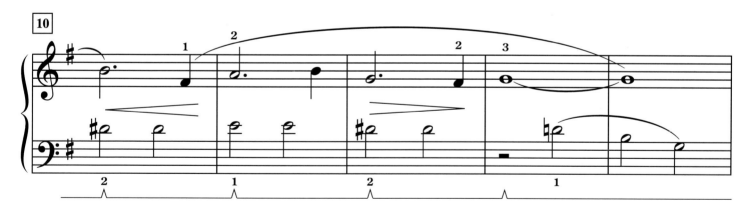

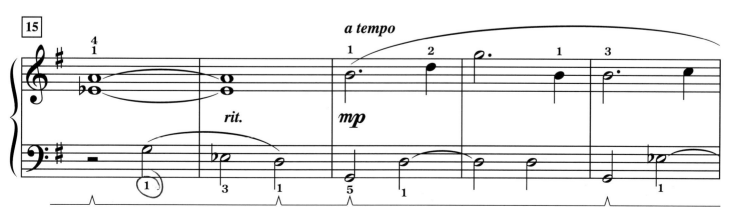

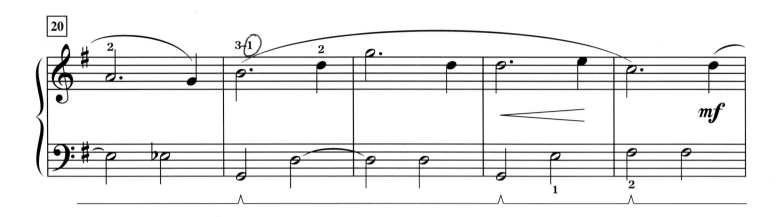

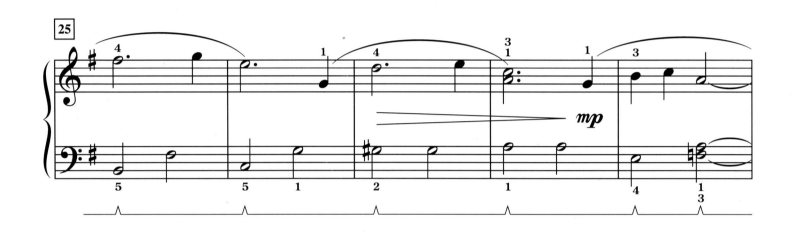

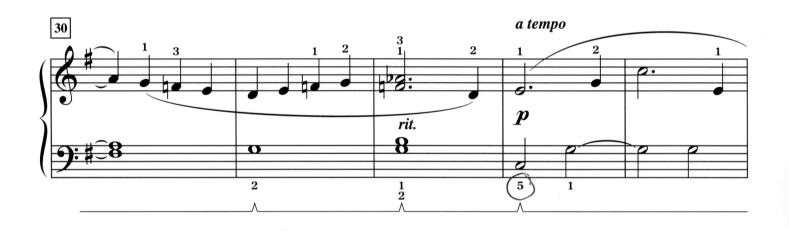

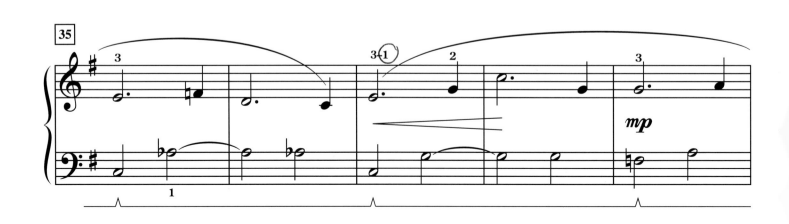

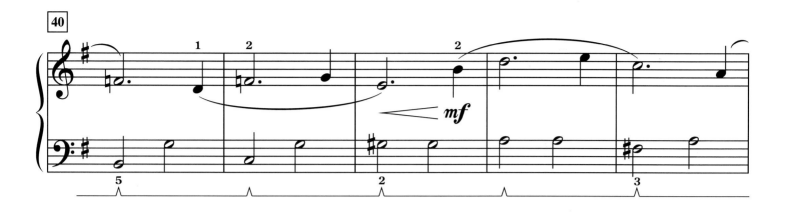

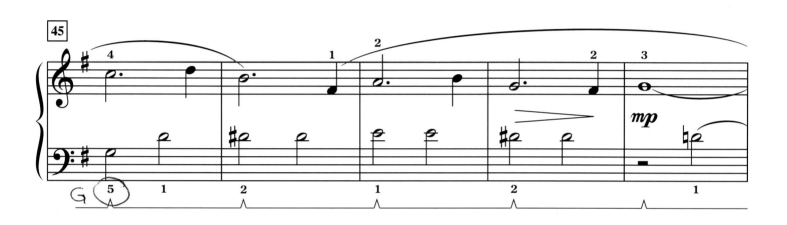

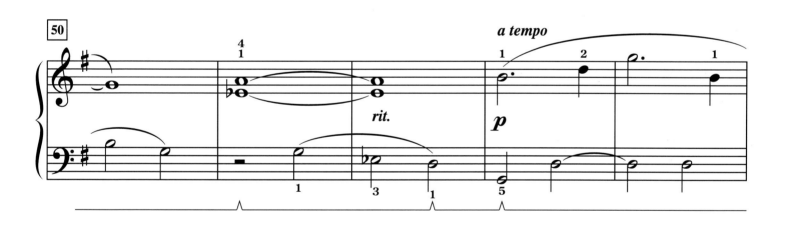

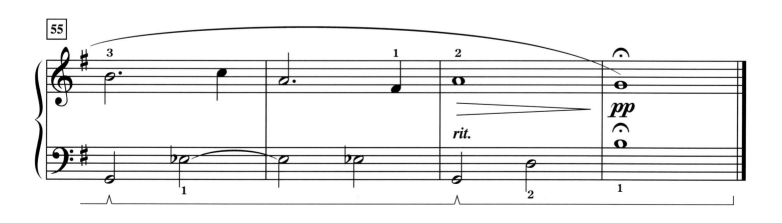

REMEMBER
(from "Troy")

Words by Cynthia Weil

Music by James Horner
Arranged by Carol Matz

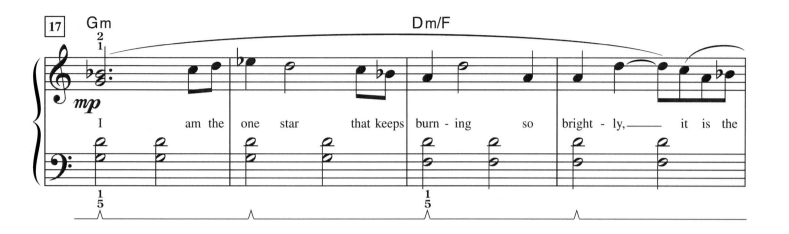

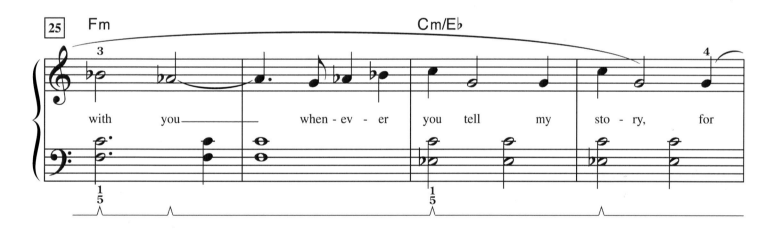

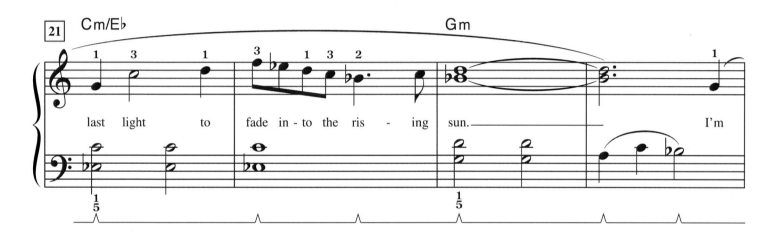

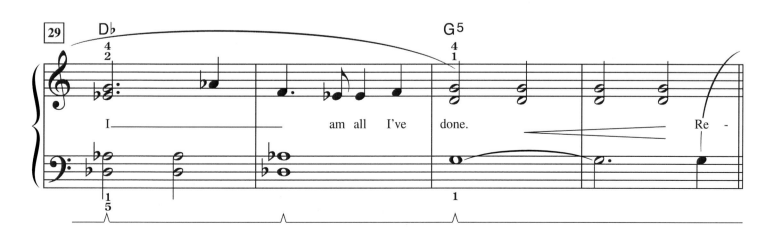

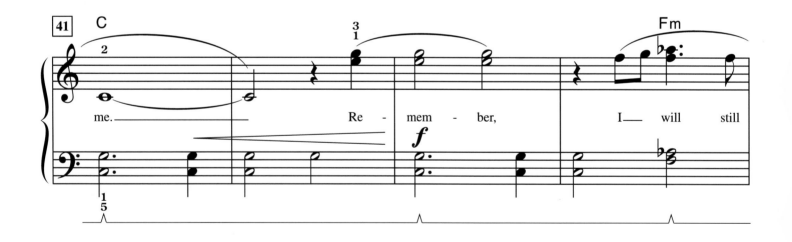

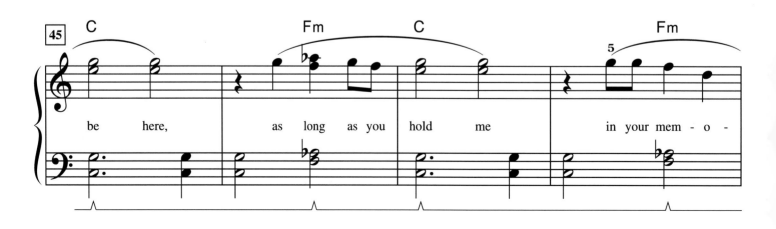

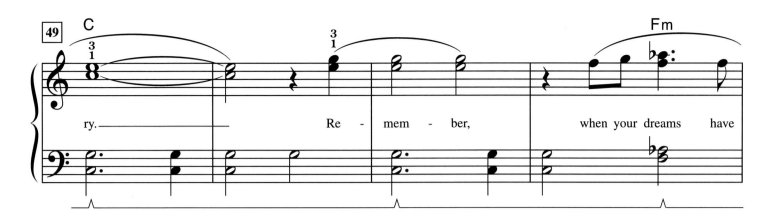

ry._____ Re - mem - ber, when your dreams have

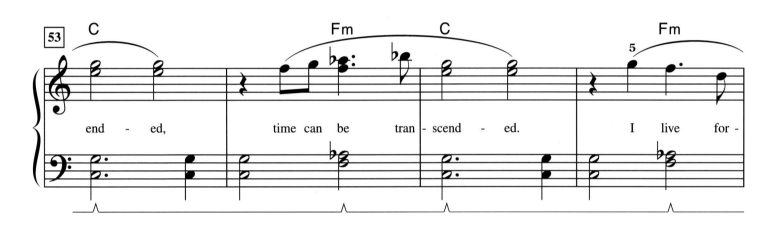

end - ed, time can be tran - scend - ed. I live for-

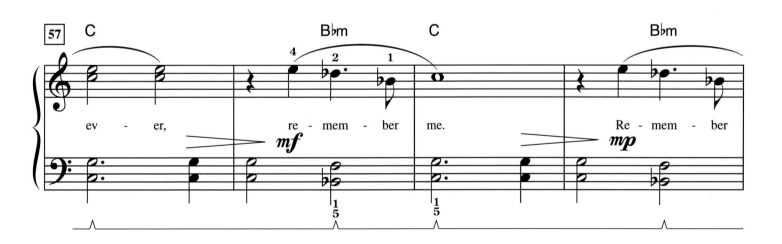

ev - er, re - mem - ber me. Re - mem - ber

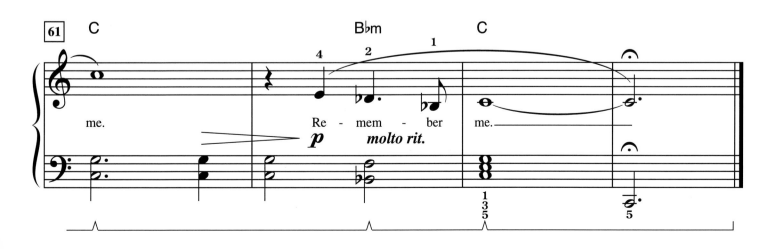

me. Re - mem - ber me.____

STAR WARS®
(Main Title)

By **JOHN WILLIAMS**
Arranged by Carol Matz

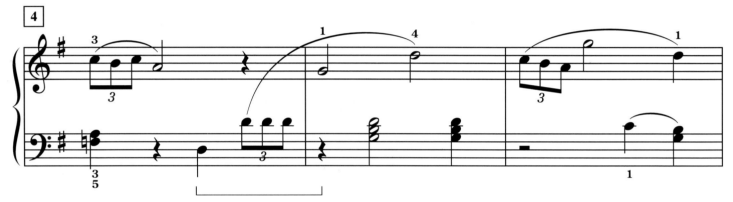

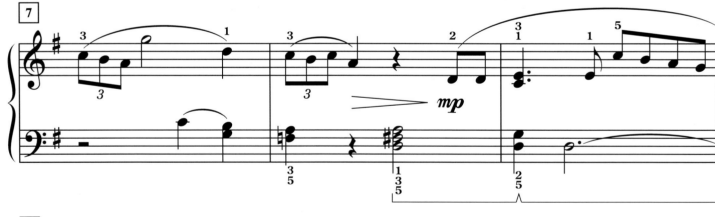

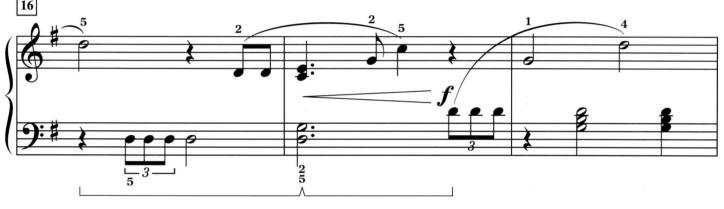

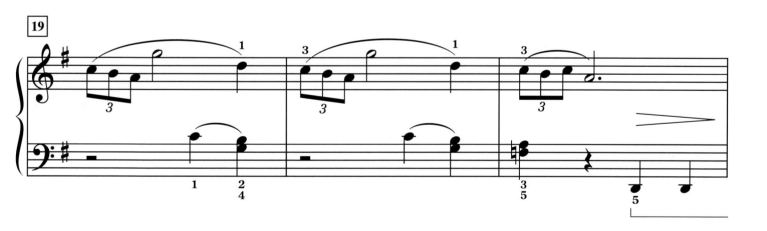

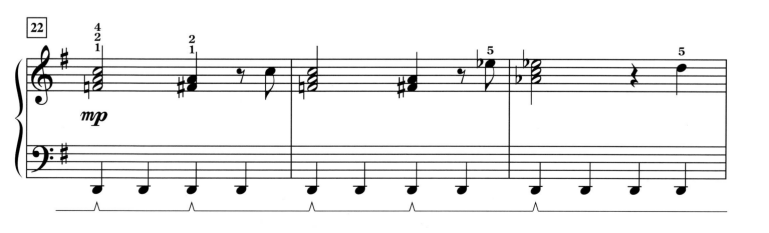

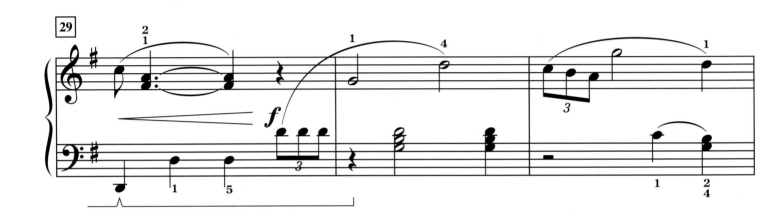

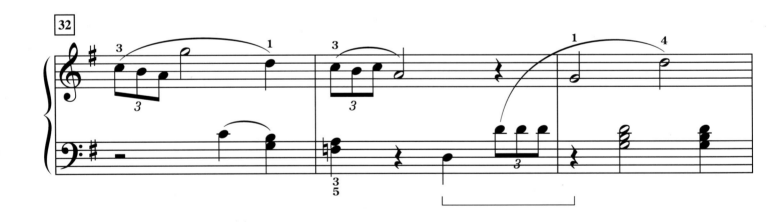

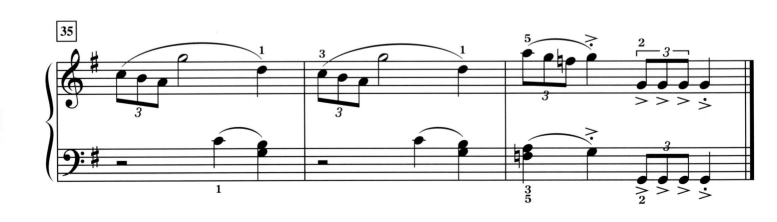

WONKA'S WELCOME SONG
(from "Charlie and the Chocolate Factory")

Lyrics by John August and Danny Elfman

Music by Danny Elfman
Arranged by Carol Matz

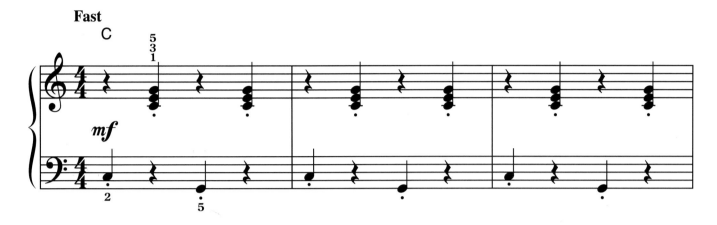

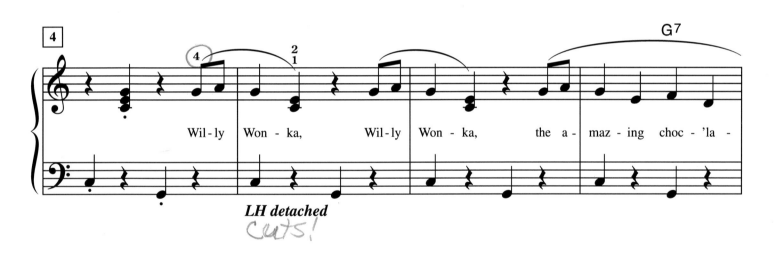

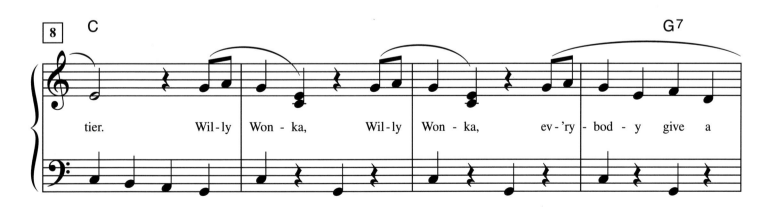

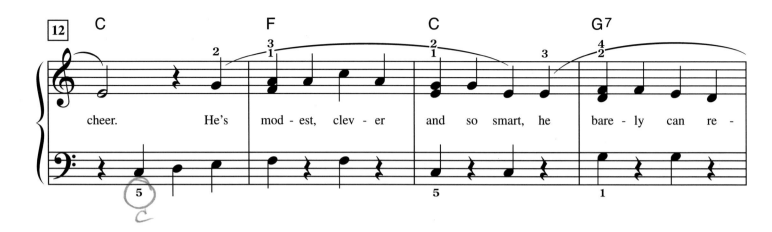

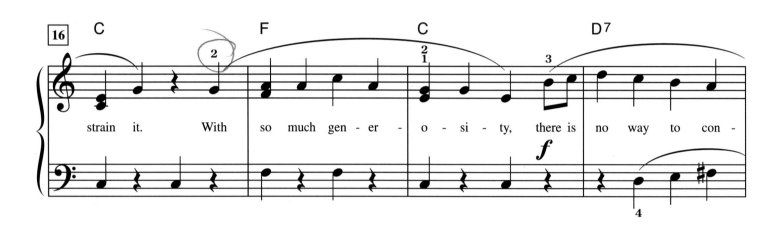

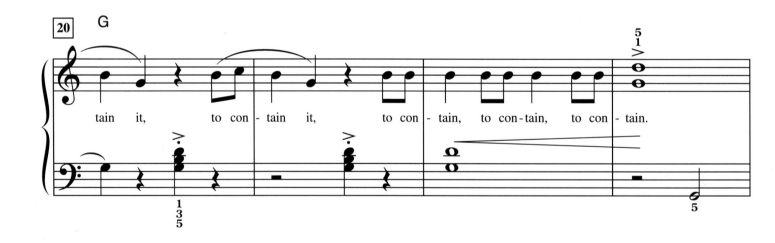

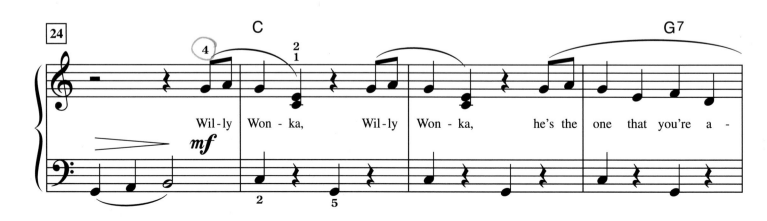

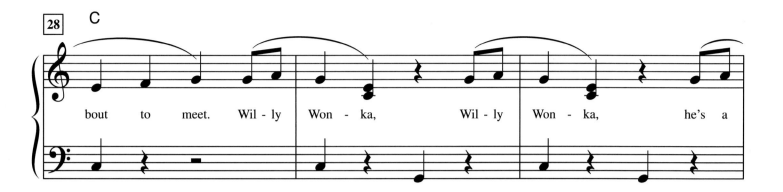

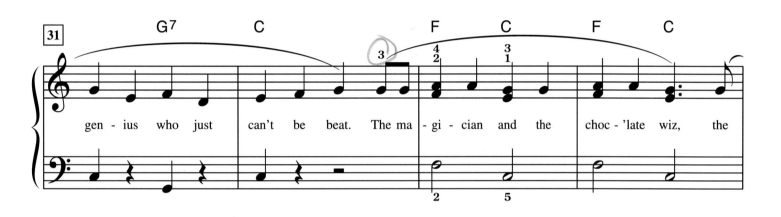

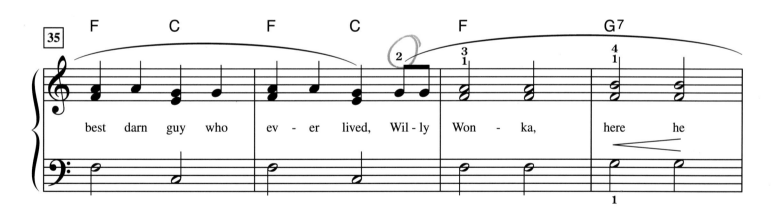

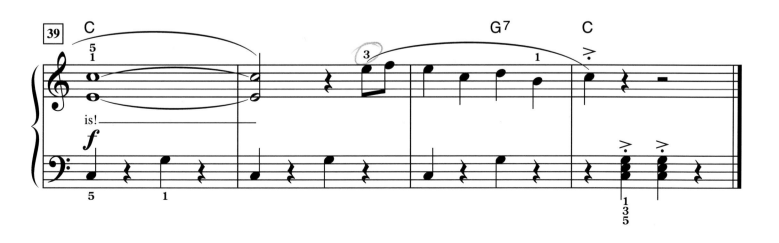